Cra Shopping

🪁 Dominie Press, Inc.

Crabby Cat went shopping.
"This cart is too short!"

"This bread is too long!"

3

"This fish is too small!"

"This meat is too big!"

"This can is too heavy!"

"This balloon is too light!"

"This milk is just right!"